WAITING FOR SNOW
IN LEWISTON

POEMS

by

Augustine Towey, C.M.

Lewiston Poetry Series
Volume 11

The Edwin Mellen Press
Lewiston●Queenston●Lampeter

Library of Congress Cataloging-in-Publication Data

Towey, Augustine.
   Waiting for snow in Lewiston : poems / by Augustine Towey.
      p. cm. -- (Lewiston poetry series ; v. 11)
   ISBN 0-88946-892-3
   I. Title. II. Series.
PS3570.O89W35 1990
811'.54--dc20   90-34542
                                                        CIP

This is volume 11 in the continuing series
Lewiston Poetry Series
Volume 11 ISBN 0-88946-892-3
LPS Series ISBN 0-88946-894-X

Edited by Patricia Schultz

The Edwin Mellen Press
Box 450   Box 67
Lewiston, New York   Queenston, Ontario
USA 14092   CANADA L0S 1L0
                  The Edwin Mellen Press, Ltd.
                    Lampeter, Dyfed, Wales
                  UNITED KINGDOM SA48 7DY

Printed in the United States of America

This book is for my Mother,
Anne M. Towey

Contents

Poems for The Dearest

Other Poems

Acknowledgements

Some of these poems have appeared in *The Commonweal, Talon, The Aquila, The Buffalo Courier-Express, The Buffalo News,* and *The Niagara Gazette.*

The author gratefully acknowledges the generous assistance of Dr. Sharon O. Watkinson, department of theatre studies, Niagara University; Dr. John Stranges, Academic Vice-President, Niagara University; and Patricia Schultz, The Edwin Mellen Press.

Poems for The Dearest

"I am so busy . . ." (Isaiah 11:1-10)

I am so busy that I forget to remember I am happy.
So I recall the miracle.
                    I was cold.
Even the trees were shivering. In a field
Somewhere between Youngstown and Lewiston
I saw a wolf, a leopard, a lamb, a kid,
A neighborly bear browsing, and a cobra singing
For the lamb. A lion spectacularly groomed
Dusted the doorstep for the kid; the wolf announced
The eagle's arrival (who came with a dove on his arm);
The child brought the adder. There
Was even a swan unfolding wings and messages.
There was even a shooting star.
O the lengths the heavens will take.
"Tomorrow I shall wake up happy."
We shall all wake up happy, I thought:
Lion, kid, lamb, adder, child, and swan.

"I sometimes think . . ."

I sometimes think I come to you
the way my students read poems;
full of interpretations,
they force the flower from the rose,
the planet from the moon,
and the earth goes out of the garden.
I interpret you.
But you are all literal.
In heaven, where you come from,
there are no supreme fictions.
You are no metaphor, no mirror,
no analogy, no simile, no equation.
Desiring the exhilaration of changes,
the ambiguous moon, the imagined garden, the untouchable rose,
burning with wit and novelties,
I see afresh and do not see.
I alter you with metaphor.
O world without meaning
in the blessed first and last of things
together and one and never something other!
O dearest virtual,
I am grateful
you are no irony.

"Dearest, my maker . . ."

Dearest, my maker of inconsequential miracles,
gracious, ingenuous sovereign of small talk,
could you spare me some moments of exclamation,
some afternoon, perhaps, write me a second act?

Any crisis, dear, will do:
let the fires burn out, the trees give no shade,
and the gardens be overgrown.
Let the gates be closed and the kissing time be over,
let the colors of flowers fail,
and knots be undone, let the clocks wind down,
let clouds be bricks and mortar turn to taffy.
Let all reversals multiply!
Let weeds be garlands, ant hills be mansions,
and everyday all day be Sunday mornings.

But just for an afternoon.
Then, dear, restore the gardens and clocks,
the kissing and clouds,
Bring back the weeds and small talk
so I may wonder at your wonder.

"Dearest, I settled the other week . . ."

Dearest, I settled the other week into a day of ordinary autumn.
Driving to East Aurora where the trees were on fire,
arching over us, their fire falling for shade,
the asphalt gold, the hills at a distance benign, restrained,
we searched for roadside pumpkin stands; found none.
Passing the signs "Deer X-ing," I prayed,
show me, give me a deer to make this day.

Then on to our friends; the fire of trees brought
into the house, their daylight burning beneath the mantel.

Twilight: before dinner a drive through the country,
watching the trees fail, the hills blue out.

Dusk: then out of the dark he flew,
bounding from the thicket to the road like a whippet through
        weeds,
then poised in our path, seized by the lights of the car,
he stared us down.
this fragile, precarious, miraculous bright fawn.

"So here now, dear one . . ."

So here now, dear one,
now this delight is gone.
This safe island that you had
is broken by my storms,
this cove you chose to harbor in,
this place you shared against your enemies.
(you, dear one) is rife with thieves,
filled, still abandoned.

Here now, dear one,
now this delight is gone.

I am your thief,
I am your abandonment.

And you, my gardener and my friend,
you till me every good gift,
you tell me all best news,
I cannot (try hardest, I do),
I cannot mend myself:
keep me in your patience,
do not be alarmed,
so I may meekly
here now, dear one,
turn myself home.

So, so, so.

First Snow with Orange

The necessities of life, dearest,
I think of them this morning standing
on the campus lawn early in the first snow
and ponder life without embellishment
like a poem without metaphor.

The lawn seems stretched by the snow,
one vast unruffled reach,
with seven trees like interpoints to lend the lawn perspective.
The trees are undercapped with orange,
a residue from yesterday's autumn.
(For a moment I think the orange is an extra).

In this whiteness to divine the essential
seems an appropriate task.
What is necessary? My radical boots
and scarf? great green coat? my cigarettes?
Suddenly flakes on my eyeglass blur, soften the scene
like movies in the forties filmed through gauze.

Which, then, ornaments the view: eyeglass? myself?
or that my first pious (actually romantic) thought
is that you alone suffice to shape this moment into what it is?
I want nothing you can not bring me by coming alone.

So I stand thinking of you
in this snowscape like moonscape
and my meditation makes you present
as if I clicked a button on a slide machine
and the next view, a duplicate of the first
with you now in it, filled the screen.

The new light swarms around your head.
The trees, for reverence, have nearly shed
their bleakness and assume this light into their snow.
Your figure, encased in amethyst and morning red,
perfects the morning, singing your sweet hello.

I know no probable reason, dearest,
why we should stand in this lawn,
inevitable and necessary to the scene
and to each other; no, nothing reasonable.
But here, now, I think for the moment
I could live in this snow forever.

Absconditus

Dearest, I walk in the rain this afternoon
and turn a familiar corner, expecting you.
A dead-weight rain dropped out of the sky last night
as though the huge water balloon of night were punctured;
leaves fell from trees like a thousand Icarus.
A wet leaf drags at my heel, my Wallabees are soaked,
my pants' legs flap like twin flags unfurled.
I look for you. You are not here.

There are vacancies I never imagined;
turning a corner, taking a path, the special
corner, the favorite tree, the place between trees,
the teddy bear, the book, your book, the window,
the singular music, the hallway to the window,
the red seat in a row of red seats,
the grey wall where the vine is autumn red.

O for your love now here in the thick of it,
smiling at me across a din of other faces,
startled again by grace and cheer, awaiting
the glorification of tree, of grove, of book, of bear.
I know my present loss is only a sense of loss,
a trick of memory, a lack of persistence
as in prayers not said or letters never written;
I know that which is hidden from that which is gone.
                    Dearest,
this is just to say I love you sanely
despite my panic
this afternoon of frantic rain and disappointment.

Waiting for Snow

I have nothing to write you this morning. This early
There are no universals. A mongrel scuddles by,
The leaves skim on the walk. On television
There is talk of snow in the afternoon.

I shave and finish shaving and go down
To breakfast. I take my coffee and lean against
The doorsill, smoking idly, as the dog goes past
And one leaf falters as if about to speak.

On the table I admire the clean prose
Of DiCamillo bread, sliced once, the one
Slice fallen, crumbs trailing in triads from the board
To the facets the sunlight flails through the marmalade jar

Across the white cloth and over the honey dish.
I admire the conventions of breakfast and the spare
Perfection of its innocent combinations:
Bread, marmalade and crumbs, and wish

I had something to write you this morning, this early.
Dearest, this afternoon's snow may speak more clearly.

The Advent

I have prepared for your coming what I can prepare.
I've cleared my desk of business and my heart
Is empty. Tests are graded and whatever part
Of me possible stands ready as if on a stair.

I will come down to greet you at the door.
Until then I've balanced budgets and my gifts
Are wrapped. I've tried to settle any rifts
I know of. I'll hear you on the porch's broken floor.

I've shoveled the walk of snow till it is bare,
And if no other storms occur I should
Be safe. A single deer at the edge of the wood
Stomps and stares. Nights have been colder, but days fair.

I've set aside what might encumber your stay.
My calendar is free of lunches, meetings.
There is none left to whom I must send greetings.
Dearest, all that remains is that you find your way.

Feuilles Mortes

This is autumn's ugliest day; the trees
Are stripped. The few leaves that cling
To the ground are khaki. Nearly grey clouds are formless
Where there are any, and the grey of clouds and sky
Is the grey of tin, hollow and unyielding.

I remember another afternoon of grey skies
That gave way after a mottled start
To a cerulean diaposan, and the stammel leaves
On the lawn, abundant, prosperous, and magical.
You walked stocking-footed that afternoon,
An urchin, picking up leaves, gave me some,
And then, Orlando-like, placed the others
Back among the branches.
"They'll never stay," I said. "Never,"
You answered. "Never meant to. Meant to fall
In the first place — or second place." You laughed.
Then you crushed others in your hand and
          threw them like confetti
Into the air, a fine rain of powdered maple.
A leaf (not one of yours) fell by itself.
"Look, I told you — meant to fall."
But, you, dearest, I believed the leaves would stay for you,
Find sap and strength a second time, another spring.
On this barest day I wish for you, I wish for leaves,
For you to re-affix among the skeletons of trees.

The Lovers and the Christ of Compunction
Summer, 1988

I sit on a picnic bench outside the house
On a cool mid-August evening, and watch the cars
Glide by. The summer's traffic, thick with tourists,
Has trickled out, and curls around the bend
Of Hyde Park Blvd. and Lewiston Rd.,
Slow, intermittent and lazy, like a column
Of lost ants. I am lazy, a little lost, out of it.

The terrible heat of July and early August had passed
Through the Northeast like some relentless passion
Through a great body. This cool night
Is a relief, an open space in which
To breathe. The air is free. I breathe.

No more than fifteen yards away, two lovers
Pass, their arms intertwined. They do not see
Me. What have I to do with them, the young
In one another's arms? His rabbit nose
Nuzzles her neck. She giggles, moans a little.
He whispers something, she answers, "Yes,
Yes!" She thinks she's Molly Bloom.

They're headed for bed and a tangle of promises.
Buttressed by moonlight, he swears, "I'll never
Hurt you." She wears his assurance on her lips
Like lipstick. Nothing matters to them but them.
But what have I to do with them? I turn
Away. The stars are poised and scattered through
The leaves like snowflakes, as if winter could not wait.
I will be more lonely before I will be less.

O Christ of compunction desolate in your tree,
Favor us with your rich emptiness,
Be you the conjunction of lover and lovers,
Let the waiting stars fall from the trees and this
Cool night pass into some other tomorrow.

Autumn Carol

Sometimes the sun in the evening sits in the sling
Of the gorge like a shin-buster in the wings of a stage.
Then are the shadows of leaves like the shadows of giants,
Long like El Greco bodies, and their brown-gold is backlit
By ochre. The leaves stand on their stems like little
Umbrellas where the wind has dropped them, their backs
Cupped to the wind, to the light. The shadows of grass
Cross, cover and shade the sidewalks like sable.
The yearling maple, leafless, fingers its way
Two stories up a building's stone wall, and the stones'
Shadows themselves curve around the mortar.
The fallen twig of a hawthorne stretches across
The entire length of the pathway like a stalking Giacometti.

For a time this light lingers, and all these protractions hold.
Then is the world translated into this hour of longeur
And still expectancy. Then with a sudden silent
Bump, the sun falls into the gorge. Then, dearest,
Is the world blue-grey, the leaves suck back
Their shadows, and in an instant the hawthorne,
The maple, and the grass pull in their brilliant
     brief appendices.

Other Poems

Lines Based Upon a
Meditation by Thomas Traherne

O you are meant for love
As the sun is to shine, and without it you are useless
    And as dark as the spent fire.
    And the whole world ministers to you
As the theatre of your love. It nourishes you
And every object so you may continue to love them.
    Without them you were better not to live.
Life without objects is sensible emptiness,
    And that is a greater misery than death or nothing.

    Consider a world without objects.
First of all, the trees: an empty field bereft of grass
    And root and trunk and branches and leaves.
On what might the snow fall, or the rain,
    (If there were snow or rain?)
And where would green adhere if not in the grass or tree,
    And orange and red in the ripe leaf,
    And brown in the bark?
For autumn lives in the dying tree and winter in
    The down of snow upon branches.
So, winter and spring go from the barren hill
    Or field, barren of season then since
Spring, summer, winter, fall live in the trees.
    How could you face the uniday of their absence?

19

Then consider, say, the absence of the violin or flute.
Where is Mozart or Bach, or Berlin or Strouse? Where
    Is the music that you love? What would become
    Of dancing? We would keep time by clapping
And sing unaccompanied forever. Music is in the objects
        Of musicians and the throats of singers
As the wind is only in a tunnel or the canyon of skyscrapers.
    Music is in the notes of the score and the strings
    Of the fiddle and the bow in the hand of the fiddler
        And your singing.

        And then the silver frame
That holds the photo. Gone, both the photo and the frame.
    Then where is, what encompasses the souvenir?
Your recollection cannot contain the moment as the photo
    Cannot contain your thoughts but both together
Recollect all that was ever lived or breathed or spoken
        Between us. There in
    Its lively stillness the photo in the silver frame
Sustains your love, as Piero della Francesca reveals
The family of things in the objects of his paintings
        And the painting of objects,
In the guise of the separateness of ordered outer things
Where the poetry of deep affinities is identical
        With those objects.

        O you are meant for love
And all the objects of the world are yours
    As the bow is for the fiddle, and
    The trees are for the seasons, and the frame
Is for the photo, and this poem is
    An object among them too.

                        (Read at the wedding of
                        Mary Cleere Haran and Joe Gilford.)

20

Lapis Lazuli

I would to have shut you in a dungeon
(like a prize),
a luxurious dungeon, of course,
a jail of comforts and delights,
a prison of attention.

There would be a window looking on a willow.
This willow would be green
and would not lean as much as others,
not a sad tree,
and underneath its hidden bark
a clean stream, silent for sleeping,
but in the morning like a rooster,
and near the stream remarkable flowers.

In the furthest corner a small orchestra
of flutes, reeds and viols,
a stuffed pheasant on a cedar sideboard,
two crystal vases in which I'd fix a strange arrangement
of roses, wheat, and fern. You'd learn
to love them and the gramaphone,
the three stuffed bears, the spindle, and the clock
(inscribed from Chaucer, "Amor vincit omnia.")
A tiffany lamp, the only one meant to be lighted.

For recreation, billiards, monopoly, and backgammon,
children you might dance with: learned and wise and something
        shy,
they'd twist and pas de trois and monkey,
home-made movies by Fellini,
one ancient, prized, imperishable doll,
its head half off and one leg missing,
a small oak cross for kissing.

The roof, a plastic geodesic dome
to keep the weathers out, the seasons in,
by the door near the corner
a precious plant of green and gold
(I'd find it in the East)
its leaves like little fans and every blossom different.
You'd hear it breathe at night.

And nearby the sea, booming.

Sometimes the thunder for a difference.

And I would come to you in the evening
when the orchestra had left,
down a dark corridor, past other rooms
whose doors I'd shut and lock,

And I would tell you as explicitly as possible
the way this dungeon was my heart.

(For Paula-Jo and Pete Gunther)

Marriage

We praise usually what we can see:
the felicitous phenomenon,
as in some scape to the horizon,
or in the museum or the open air
pears counterpoised symmetrically
on the neat white cloth upon the table,
cadences shimmering testily over words,
Euclid's dazzling arrival.
But here we are forced to praise
what is invisible
and see by light of promises.
We can admire marriage's apparent virtues—
courage, faith like fire,
indisputably Pauline,
this trust in things unseen,
this trust in things to come,
this double martyrdom.

But what is unapparent
is wisdom's child.

These dangerous allies,
alliances, domestic treaties,
no, really foreign contracts,
which, in their disregard for logic
where process and result are equivalent
and there are no surprises,
seen impertinent and to reason's admonitions
downright rude;
it is joy giving way to grief,
it is madness,
it is insane,
it is dangerous,
it perishes with the perishable
and runs the risk of rust.

23

Why bother, then, why fuss?
it has of all our inventions
the look of eternity
(and the promise, we might add)
notwithstanding Bennett's admonition,
that its horror is its dailiness.
We say, its challenge, too, for the courageous,
if their hearts are large enough
and have esprit.
Its truth lies in its ability to test,
this crucible of the quotidien,
without the need for proof.

If a wife is a coffin
and possession is the grave of love,
we might remember too
that a religion may begin with the resurrection.
Its beauty is impractical,
even disregarding the romantical;
yet all the while it makes of art
a thing most serviceable,
in the sense that one might sell
a poem for an urn.
It is spontaneous initial originality,
and takes as warning what
Stravinsky said of pitch:
'If for some reason I transpose it,
I am in danger of losing the freshness
of first contact,
and will have difficulty in recapturing
its attractiveness.'

She is perfection
(now only in his reflection,
but she will become in ours, in time,
a valiant universal)
but she is perfection
she is the sound of a flute
the mystery of water rising and the boat
rising with it, the ebb and flow
the rise and fall
the involuntary mystery, the voluntary given,
she is the sound of a flute
the thin cool line which plays warm melodies
she is all seasons
which open and close upon each other
she is distance and closeness
leaving, returning
she is, more negatively,
no angel,
happily.

Of him, we say
we know a real man when we see him.
Concentration, brevity, interest, are some
of the virtues he wears smilingly, but not grinningly.
The face is kindly, above all:
an aspect of something interior, we would say
more metaphysically, and ask then, as he smiles,
'teach us the manner of silence and composure.
I mean that genuine silence deep down
after the wind has nuzzled the trees
and basted the water, silence where we may
in recollection hear the sound again
and name it. Then when we've pronounced it,
we've got it, and may smile ourselves.'

His concern is loving,
a sensitivity at once gracious and immune.
He vaccinates with sugar cubes where resiliency is lacking
and where possible, he encourages the necessary armor.
A healthy humour sancitfies his counsel.
Need it be said, after all,
some find his best counsel in his own example?

Well, we are grateful for these tall persons,
As a Canadian woman wrote (to NASA
after it had launched its first satellite)
"Thank you for making us look up."
And inward, I might add.

Dialogues for a Wedding
for Susan's Marriage with Hugh

Go on, go
on. The sparrow, is it?—
No, not the nightingale
    (Oh where, where are the nightingales
      these evenings?)—
the everyday sparrow or the commonplace robin
    sings (speaks? whistles?),
    Go on, do it.
    Leap, match and marry
    if your hearts are in it.

We smile as you say,
    "It is not merely a matter of being consoled,
      but of being completed.
For example, we took the boat to the center
    of the lake
    as a divertisement (well, no, it was more);
    it was pleasing in the heavy afternoon; we felt
      relieved.
    But the going back, while we enjoyed
      the talk and company,
    the going back had the quality of necessity.
    Like the other side of the mountain,
    or the same side, coming down."
Well, we understand these similes and smile
      again
    hearing the sparrow, the encouraging bird,
    and the unreasonable risk we rune
    from his warble (tune?)
Look, have you an idea of it?

We admonish in expectancy, you understand,
    but like Miss Marianne's student's life, we'd say
      in caution,
    this nesting "is beset with dangers,
      mildews, complaisancies,"
    Admittedly, this great convention
      buckles
    at your personal invention;
    you monogram this institution
    (like some book of which others own
    the same edition, but your copy is your own).
Forgive us if at this celebration we wonder privately,
    Is it fidelity
    which seems so admirable because
      so perilous?

You say,
    "Like steel,
    exposed.
      (Others are in monuments
      and speak to other virutes: justice, honor
      courage, brave deeds.
      Statues, obelisks with eagles atop,
    their feathers choreographed,
      heads in dramatic precision west or east,
      cast there in beauty perhaps—
      perhaps, but cold.
      Virtue is comfortless and stoic there.
      If their heroes spoke, they'd say,
      The deed had to be done,
      we did it, and carried on.)"

But this will have to be
like steel exposed,
    running the risk of rust.
Faithful to what design? There is none.
    What we vow, we vow privately
    and let you hear our intimacy.
We'll make assurances as we meet the tears that need
      mending.
    We smile too and hear the sparrow.
      Like steel
      exposed, we say,
    "This is imperishable,
    this will not yield."

Poem from Ireland

There are some things I've noticed today
and tried to memorize:
petal of violet near a sunflower stalk;
leaves upon stone like amateur moss
(the wind will take them,
though my eyes have kept them,
though my eyes have stayed them);
a white jar spilt on its side,
oozing an orange marmalade;
and the pale curtains in Ireland,
which bloused through the window that evening,
came back today, that evening, that evening;
crumbs on the teakwood breadboard;
a pine, two elms, and a maple
all in a row on a dark horizon.
Listen, these are for you. Complete them.

Four Christmas Letters

How many goodly creatures are there here.
               The Tempest

          1.
At the age of six I thought a mirror held
against a backwards script which
righted in reflection
a miracle.

Now you say I am your mirror,
and I learn how
exhausting
a miracle can be.

2.

I have to write you this to say
we have no common ground,
but trudge back and forth
inventing a landscape.
Invention: Our plotting corridors
and sympathies of conversation.
We make a house without a cellar.

Imagine we picnic on a legend of lawn
beneath a trunkless tree. If you want, there are ants.
Clouds come, the sun goes in, and it rains.
Or: it rains, the sun comes out, clouds disappear.
Variety of the possibilities of syntax.

We are like mice in a labyrinth,
thinking a door where there is none.
We stump our heads and start again.
This maze of our design is neither
less nor more than other ravels.
We'll learn in time the exits,
memorize the passage-ways
and come to run it
in a minute.
                That dull day
let us disappear,
even from each other.
Tell me (now that it's your turn)
what do you say?

3.

In a Christmas snapshot (you are six or seven and
jaded uncles and aunts engulf you)
smiling, your face leans out,
hair lacquered, nose and forehead scrubbed to
shine, you look prepared for
miracles, as if the camera's shutter should
click some Santa Claus or Eden into
view. The snapshot petrifies expectancy
and with grotesque suspense refuses
answers. What in these years between
your frozen nervous grin and my regard
unlocked your smile, made Eden out of
love's unlit caves?
                  Did you see, at six
or seven, who was taking the photograph?

4.

That
communion where my praise
was lipservice
impeccable,
and the throaty hymn
swollen to an immaculate reverence,
the feathered perfect syllables
flew to a taxidermist god.

Now you and this communion
where I sweat and bleat
irreverences, fumble,
I cough
inchoate gestures and
abandon them.

Take my fumble.
It's Christmas.

At the River Near the Power Vista

Not to have technique
is to carry ice in a quilt in July:
ideas are that perishable;

to lack style
is to gavotte to a minuet
or finger-tap to Purcell's "Dido and Aeneas."
You've got the idea, privately.

Although to lack love,
having technique and style,
is to hatch the egg and kill the chick inside.

Psalm

Praise the green water near the powder beach
where jaguars, sleek
and harmless, yawn their psalms
monotonous beneath a hedge of cypresses
which edge the sand like figureheads. Beyond,
the formal garden's mauve expanse of lawn
prepares as if for tennis. On the hill, above,
a stately home stands; mind you, just stands:
no chimney smoke, no face or bustle behind curtains.
And then behind the lawn, the
streets of the town row after row,
row upon row,
like children's blocks without
spelling letters, hide
their foundations of hills
which now to our eye
is just a parabola of green.
Praise this diversion.

Meditation for Christmas, 1981

Paul. Ephesians 4:17-32.

I must no longer live
in the futility of my mind,
old ragpicker, fustian busybody
shuffling in the owl-light of half-ideas,
coughing at strangers for attention,
useless dogpatch where the sun goes down on my anger,
heart in chains, eyes of the heart absconded,
heart of the mind abandoned,
walk careless, speech foolish,
melodies like catarrhs,
when my words should be servants
not cataphracts,
my days friends and brothers,
not thieves,
nearly hearing the musty clamor
of mind only mine only,
at best like the cawing of gulls
(at best).

Model-T of a word-maker, image-monger,
I'm broke.

Scavenger friend, here is the refuse
your impartiality may salvage.

Ten Rhymes

Precisely at the left corner of your mouth
there is warm honey.
And I will have it.

At the back your hair is moss and brown,
unripe until
it falls.

When your hands speak
and stutter about a touch,
I will still them.

Even your mouth persists
in spelling you out.
I would learn your alphabet.

Whatever sorrow livened you
into this unfolding,
my praise might contain it.

Here is a pebble. It is round
and smooth and infinite.
It is inferior.

If I rejoice in the morning,
minding the sea and the snow,
I'll make a sadness of it.

When the landlady asked my address
and her husband sanded the eccentric steps,
you persisted.

After your sleep, at your waking, I imagine
your second sleep; and your statue
is empty of all of you.

I've seen you cry
and it
is witty.

Poem for My Student

To start
I would wish
an extravagance
of tenderness,
the solvent shards
of feeling.

After rain,
the clear air to hover
like a tent
over a valley
of vegetation.

The hand promised
and given:
an improvised
salute to leaven
stone or rock, whatever.

And many hands
ears lips eyes
fingers not his
to feel all feelings out
not his.

If we "will die of cold,
not darkness,"
I would wish
a fever.

Finally,
a failure of words,
of light; dumb
before heaven,
free from us,
dark in his freedom.
the last syllables:
unnecessary.

But to start
a green thumb
on the valley
of his heart.

A Poem for Certain Children of My Former Students

Some of your parents
in a photo on my desk
smile through colors which your births would bleach.

They're six there, three
over three, two lines
of faces grouped as though the combination would last,

communal posture
in collective portrait
during a year my celibate love could entertain them.

As if a peacock's fan
folded suddenly
something collapsed the hour you shouldered in for keeps.

Their pleasasnt faces frozen
in belief assume there
still the giant lies they read in lines of heady verse.

The truest lie
was Lear's
who once assembled daughters, friends, fools

in primitive
daguerreotype
to catalogue and keep his love's strength three by three.

History records
other combinations:
time once made subtractions from thirteen
and left one hanging between

two. Of these
one blanched,
the other gathered to the first and he began again.

Smile, children,
in ensemble.
My wishes are not cruel and great lies never crumble.

Night Walk

It goes somewhere in a narrow music
of much pause and interval;
the notes' breaths have it,
cough and sigh,
cough and sigh;
so small the melody (at most four notes)
but intricate,
a filigree;
and hearing it behind a door,
you'd think a child were playing;
not Czerny, but
four fingers of its hand
at random;
the start and stop
so vacant,
all repose;
except the strike is sure,
the interval is clearer.

Song

for Pris and John's wedding,
sung by John who makes an
elaborate metaphor by placing
his hands, cupped, next
to her ear.

This now is how it sounds first-hand:
Five miles or more of ocean I lean
In my cupped hands against your ear.
Waves batter banks of flesh, fish
May die in the dry intersections of my fingers,
But pearls crouch in the deep shells of my palms.
Tides ache for shore. The moon,
Contained herein, crusts this cup with silver.
There are no boats: no slap
Against wood, no need for winds.
All night the gulls are silent, listening.
By day they circle, looking for rest.
There is none. They settle on white caps
Which eventually engulf them.

My hands against your ear I fashion
In my heart like a bridge,
Like a megaphone, and I speak to you
Through the sea.

I would be insular. Now,
Knowing that boats will have to come
(Gulls squatting on their sterns),
Understanding even now how we must endure
The commerce of their wakes, the industry
Of their fishing and the deep involvement of their nets.

In Memory of Heinzie. I Corinthians 15:35-49.

There never was a photograph quite like you:
most had you glowering in disco, or
petulant on bright Jamaica sands, or
smiling in graveyards, or
pouting amid a fleet of Buicks, or
swimming with sharks;

air-brushed to high-chic stardom
you never looked as if you were at home.

I have a picture of you in my head from life:
you stand on Fifth Avenue,
there is a bus, a cop,
you're wearing glasses, have freckles,
your hair is thinning,
it is Sunday morning, and Saturday night is asleep,
and anguish falls in curls above your eyes

for star differs from star in glory.

After Lear

I.

I heard in the morning, early, before the alarm,
The sounds on the boards, the uneasy shuffle,
A scurry of feet on the bare boards
Of the uncarpeted floor of the hall,
The muffled voices in the other corridor,
Like small animals with little claws,
Back and forth, running back and forth,
A faint percussive industry,
Then the dead stop of a silence,
And my breathing waiting, wanted, waited
A moment longer, and then
Distinctly, the creaking of shoes
And rustling of silk,
Trying the mount of the stairs
Just before the alarm.

II.

Mine Enemy's Dog

Curled before my fire, turns its head,
Looks at me as if to yawn or bark,
The dark tip of its tail swags along the carpet.
He raises it. His breathing seems to cease,
Then drops his head, dead still, onto his paws.

I turn back to my book. I turn a page.
The heart of the fire is nearly fallen to embers.
He has stayed there in that same coil
Longer than I had expected, now
Intimate guest, uneasy host.
What does he want besides heat and food?
When will he find his way into my kitchen?

I raise my eyes from the page.
The cur has changed position, stands
Now before me. He stares me down.

I take the dare and close my book.
I stand too. I start to leave
And without looking back to see
Wonder if he'll follow me upstairs.

Robert Croo

"Item, paid to Robert Croo for making three worlds, 3s 8d."
From the records of the Guilds which presented plays in
England in the Middle Ages. (Program note for "The Mysteries
at the Lyceum," Summer, 1985.)

God has blessed you,
Robert Croo,
Making three worlds for 3s and 8d.
Did you hesitate
Before taking the commission,
Or was it merely a refinement,
A natural progression
Of your daily profession?

And the making —
Did it haunt you, waking
And sleeping, as you drew
Three orbs against the blue?
Did they come all in a rush,
Three quick strokes of the brush?

What color did you choose
Against the blues?
Subtle or bold?
Silver or gold?
And as for the sky, what was the hue?
Sky-blue as in the English blue
After rain? Or Mary's color,
Hopeful but not without a hint of dolor?

Did it transform you, this assignment?
Did you mind about the children less and scold
Your wife infrequently? Were you more pleasant?
After the pageant and celebrity, did you return to old
Habits? Am I too personal? too bold?

But how I would like to have watched you paint them,
How I would like to have made your acquaintance.

Well, God bless you
Robert Croo,
The three worlds you made and God bless too
All makers of all plays
That brighten our worlds and fill our days.

The Annunciation of Ariel Jones

I want to tell you about Ariel Jones' "Annunciation,"
A portrait given to me by my friend Jane. I want to tell you
How Ariel Jones has taken Fra Angelico's original,
Photographed it, deepened and muted the colors, and placed
In the original a third person, a photographer.
If you know the original, he stands in the space
Where the angel's breath whispers the word and the event
To the girl. He is in front of them and looks straight out
At us. He wears a long black coat, faded blue jeans
(It appears), and over his shoulder but hanging to his side
Is a yellow duffle bag. And he wears a yellow hat
And round dark glasses which make him look a little
Like Woody Allen. Standing next to him on a tripod
Is a large camera. Its lens also stares straight out.
It is as though he happened upon the meeting of
The angel and the lady, and was so stunned
By what he saw, that he turned away from it to think
For a moment. What is there to photograph?
There was a girl, implicitly quiescent in
The consenting angle of her head, and an angel
In muted rose and pastel rainbow wings, inclining
Towards each other, lyrical and submissive
To what is passing between them. He is so stupefied,
This papparazzo of the Incarnation,
To wonder how you photograph a word. And disappointed.
Perhaps his editor has sent him to get the story.
And how he stands so straight and flabbergasted
Next to his rigid photographic apparatus. There
Is even some panic in his face.
Will the wire services pick this up?

Well, if you come to visit, come early
And spend some time with the portrait. It hangs
In my office, and it is witty, reverent and wise.

Two Arias from "The Beggars' Christmas"

JEAN-LUC (The Lame Beggar)

Run, you beggars. Run to your rich,
The rich who'll give you nothing.

AIME (The Blind Beggar)

Can't you stop? — Even on Christmas eve?

JEAN-LUC

Why should this night be any different?
A cripple's days are all the same,
A cripple's nights spent waking in pain.
I have limped through this terrible world,
Begging for coins and crusts of bread,
Like a scavenger, a lame bird hopping
Among rubble and rocks, living with rabble,
Living with pain. Always in pain, always in pain.
I remember dancing. I remember rooms
Spinning, as, I turned and turned
And never fell, and the long nights
Full of sleep, and morning bounded
Out of my bed into the walking street.
Now I curse the nights and days,
I curse the little folk full of praise
For little blessings.
And for this one good leg that deceives
Me, I curse God and all Christmas Eves.

AIME

Be quiet! Don't you fear God's judgment?

JEAN-LUC

I fear nothing.
You are lucky. You can't remember,
Blind from birth you never knew better.

AIME

But you *can* remember. I see the dark.
In my blank eyes a swan could be a raven,
In my eternal night the dawn is sunset.
There are no stars. I've thought a sponge
Was bread until I saw it with my mouth.
I've taken a precipice for a door
Until the ground came up to greet me.
All my world is my arm's length.
But I fear God's judgment, and I
Wish no man blind, and no man lame.
My hunger is my own, my eyes my own.
For years you've been my eyes. See better
Now and see the world forgivingly.

Eine Kleine Tinselschmerz Musik

Angels we have heard on high rarely
("Once" is more like it and then not clearly,)
        Wherefore your reticence?

Are your harps hung up and the singing ended
that blasted the hills where the shepherds tended?
        Why all the silence?

We'd like a little caroling this somber year,
Some of your "Glorias" and some of your "Don't Fear!"
        It's time for a reprise.

Score it for "Hosannahs" with trumpets under,
Then how about a cloud-blitz, how about some thunder
        Again above the trees?

We'll join you this time if you'll start the measure
Staccato, not legato (but at your pleasure),
        To tell the story

Of how they came to Bethlehem, how He was born,
How all your cymbals, all your timbrels couldn't keep Him warm
        This other side of glory.

Brother Augustine Towey, C.M. is director of Niagara University Theatre, the theatre studies program, and professor of theatre. He earned his Ph.D. in theatre from New York University and has done graduate work at the University of Birmingham (Stratford-Upon-Avon, England) and St. John's University (New York). For Niagara University he has directed over one hundred plays in the past twenty-five years. At Artpark he is an artistic consultant and the director of the Artpark Repertory Theatre (A.R.T) as well as having directed numerous professional productions at the Artpark theatre. He has given poetry readings under the sponsorship of the New York State Council of the Arts. Among his writings for the stage are *The Guardian* for NBC-TV network, *The Little Prince* (lyrics by Alan Jay Lerner and music by Frederick Loewe), *Edmund's Magic, The Common Room, Vincent in Heaven,* and the opera, *The Beggars' Christmas* (music by Richard Proulx). He was awarded an honorary Doctor of Fine Arts degree from St. John's University (New York), and the Medal of Honor by Niagara University.